WATCH ME DRAW

SPONGEBOB'S UNDERWATER ESCAPADES

Illustrated by Barry Goldberg

Bikini Bottom is filled with different kinds of sea creatures—sponges (like SpongeBob), starfish (like Patrick), sea snails (like Gary), and more!

Draw the seahorse!

When you finish your drawing, place the crab sticker on the opposite page!

SpongeBob is one lean, mean,
fry-cook machine. He can grill
Krabby Patties almost as
quickly as his pal Patrick
can eat them!

Draw the Krabby Patty!

When you finish your drawing, place the clock sticker on the opposite page!

SpongeBob and Patrick are always finding new ways to entertain themselves. Sometimes all they need is a big box and their imaginaaaation!

Draw the seashell!

When you finish your drawing, place the sea anemone sticker on the opposite page!

SpongeBob thinks he is a helpful neighbor.
Squidward thinks, well, differently.

Draw the flower!

When you finish your drawing, place the oyster sticker on the opposite page!

Both SpongeBob and Gary delight in discoveries! And there's nothing more delightful to Gary than finding a heaping helping of his favorite food!

Draw the rubber duck!

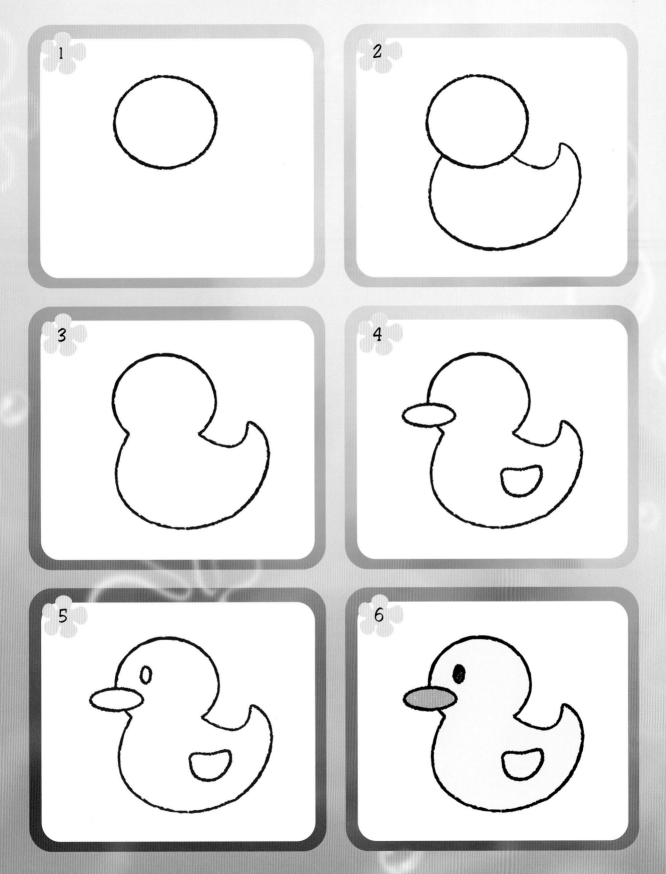

When you finish your drawing, place the picture frame sticker on the opposite page!

Sandy's treedome houses the only acorn tree in all of Bikini Bottom. In fact, it's the only tree in all of Bikini Bottom!

Draw the acorn tree!

When you finish your drawing, place the bird bath sticker on the opposite page!

One of SpongeBob's and Patrick's favorite hobbies is running around trying to catch jellyfish. Getting stung . . . well, that comes with the territory.

Draw the jellyfish!

When you finish your drawing, place the warning sign sticker on the opposite page!

Squidward is the only one who hears beautiful music when he plays his clarinet. Of course, it can be difficult to hear anything above the noise SpongeBob and Patrick sometimes make!

Draw the drum!

When you finish your drawing, place the music symbol sticker on the opposite page!

Sandy imported some familiar land creatures to keep her company in her treedome.

Draw the butterfly!

When you finish your drawing, place the snake sticker on the opposite page!

There's a reason SpongeBob hasn't passed his driving test—just ask his teacher Mrs. Puff (as soon as she's calmed down enough to answer)!

Draw the boat!

When you finish your drawing, place the anchor sticker on the opposite page!

Whenever SpongeBob and Patrick find treasure, the Flying Dutchman is never too far behind!

Draw the treasure map!

When you finish your drawing, place the ghost sticker on the opposite page!

Happy drawing!

Draw the seahorse's fin and the stripes on its tail.
Then add its eye, nose, and saddle.

Draw the Krabby Patty's bottom bun.
Then add the sesame seeds on top.

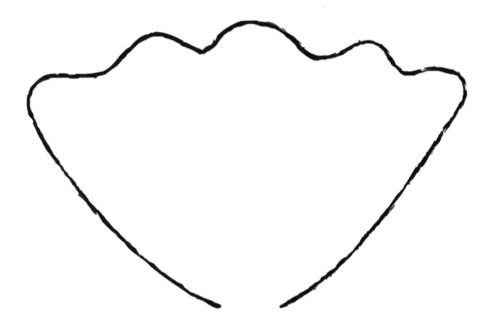

Finish drawing the squiggly base of the seashell.
Then add the diagonal lines for the ridges.

Draw a circle for the center of the flower.
Then add the stem and the leaves.

Draw the rubber duck's tail.
Then add its wing and eye.

Draw the little door on the tree trunk.
Then add the bark on the trunk, the leaves, and the acorns.

Finish drawing the jellyfish's squiggly legs.
Then add its eyes, mouth, and spots.

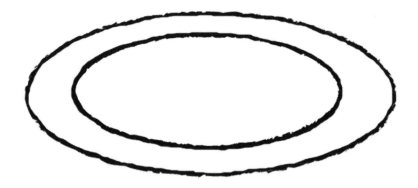

Draw the base of the drum and the drumsticks.
Then add the vertical lines on the base.

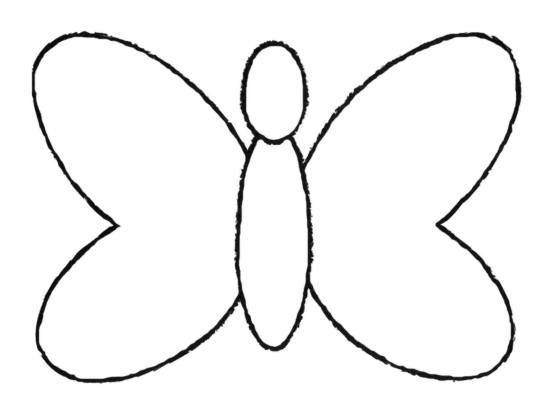

Draw the details on the butterfly's wings.
Then add the antennae.

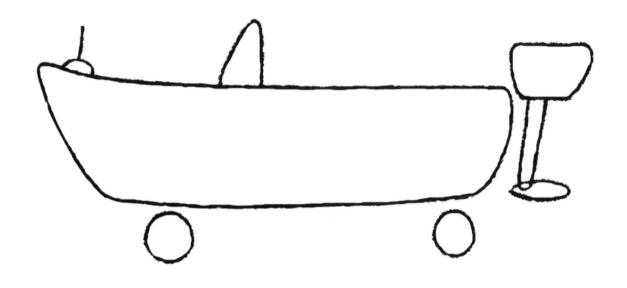

Draw the boat's door, flag, and seat.
Then finish drawing the wheels and the propeller.

Draw the X mark and the final details.
Then color the treasure map
with crayons, colored pencils, or markers.

Draw your own underwater escapade here!

DRAWING PAD